IN FLUX

By

Owen Ifill, M.D.

Copyright © 2002 Owen Ifill., MD.

All rights reserved. No part of this book may be reproduced or transmitted in any form or by any means, electronic or mechanical, including photo-copying, recording, or by information storage and retrieval system, without the written permission of the author, except where permitted by law.

Library of Congress Control Number: 2002104822

ISBN: 1-930648-32-4

First Printing, 2002

Printed in conjunction with
Goose River Press
3400 Friendship Road
Waldoboro, Maine 04572
e mail: dbenner@ime.net

In Flux

Dedication

This book is dedicated to all those who have touched my life; whether negatively or positively does not matter. It is those relationships that have seeded the experiences that have made me who I am.

I would like to especially mention my wife, Desiree; my daughter, Jessica; my mother, Inez; all of my brothers and sisters, and my extended family. I love you all.

In Flux

In flux,
at the equinox,
at the place where thought intersects
with knowing,
where time recedes,
and eternity is showing,
where life is a game that plays itself,
and love is both the means
and the reason the game is played.

In Flux

For some obscure reason,
we have scant regard for those whose convictions
change;—
for those who have a change of heart;—
for those who start seeing from a new perspective;—
for those who are bold enough
to change direction.
We respect those whose convictions never change,
however radical or ridiculous they may be.
For some obscure reason,
it hasn't occurred to us that change is natural;—
that change is healthy;—
that change is universal law;—
that change is growth;—
that inability to change is death;—
that refusal to change is anti-nature.
Change, after all,
is who we are.

In Flux

Love is nothing special;
how can something that is available to all,
at all times, at no cost, be special?
Is air special?
Love, like air, has no value.
What could you exchange love for,
when love is all there is?

***

Follow your own dreams
wherever they may lead;
the only sin there is, is allowing another,
however well meaning, to divert you;
to set our dreams adrift.
If there is one thing in your life
that you should be single minded about;
this should be it;
this is it.

In Flux

I fell down inside of me by accident,
and it was dark,
and it was chill,
and there was mist,
and there was dust,
and there were no roads
that led anywhere;
and the houses were made of cobwebs,
and time hung
from ropes of itself.
And in this room of wraiths,
I found something;
something that didn't know it was there;
something that was unconscious of its own
consciousness,
and I set it free by accident,
and it changed my life.

In Flux

Religion is a jail,
and God is freedom.
How do you seek freedom
in a jail?

***

To see truth
you need bad lenses.
Truth appears
When the world is out of focus.

In Flux

I can see why older generation blacks
can be offended by the use of the word nigga,
by our black youth;
but they need to get beyond their past
and examine reality.
Words can,
like all of relativity,
evolve.
Words mean what we want them to mean;
of themselves, they are meaningless.
The white man coined a word,
that when used,
was supposed to make us feel dirty,
feel insufficient,
feel impotent,
feel insignificant,
feel ignorant,
feel insulted.
And they,
the ghetto niggaz of this generation,
have made it into a word
that means brother,
that means friend,
that means
my man!
My souljah!
My phattest black—
that means, he who has my back.
Urban black youth have taken hate,

(continued)

In Flux

and have fashioned love
out of it;—
they have taken condescension
and made it celebration,
they have taken prejudice
and given it justice,
they have changed an insult
into a compliment,
and they are criticized for it,
they are frowned on for it,
by us!
And this they have done, in less than a generation.
This, to my mind,
is one of the great social achievements of my lifetime.
They should be applauded,
both by black and white alike.
Theirs, is a phenomenal accomplishment.
All power to you, my niggaz!
And it will come to pass
that there will come a time,
when a white man will say to a black man,
"what's up nigga?"
"Where's it happenin?"
And mean,
how is my brother?
Where is the party at?
You know what I'm sayin?
Can you feel me nigga?
Yeah!

Declare your truth,
don't worry about it.
After all,
there will always be those
to whom truth is offensive.

***

If the world were "perfect,"
you wouldn't like it,
you couldn't like it.
How do you choose
when there is no choice?
How do you play,
when there is no game?

In Flux

Do not ever expect the whole world to "love" you,
it is not possible.
Men have hated men
for simply being men.

***

What you truly believe,
is what is true for you.
What you truly believe,
is what you are currently living.
What you truly believe
is your truth.

In Flux

One of the reasons that we resent homosexual
                                                people
is their love of life;—
their fearless embrace
of life's gives and life's takes.
We resent
their joy of acceptance,
their enthusiasm,
their entrega.
We begrudge their gaiety.
If is difficult for us to
understand how people so ostracized
can be so happy;
how people who are supposedly less than us
can be happier than us.
Our consciousness
cannot wrap itself around that.

In Flux

Life means
living the hell out of it.
Love means
giving all,
and not giving a shit
about receiving a shit.
That is simply
all there is to it.

***

The problem with judging
is not judgment itself,
it is the failure to revise our judgments.
We do not double check.

In Flux

We are all addicts of one kind or another,
all of us.
Those whose addictions are not fashionable,
are the ones that are reviled,
and scorned,
and spat upon,
and made to feel like nothing.
And those of us that revile,
and scorn,
and condescend,
are not even aware that we are also addicts.
We are addicted to the feel we feel
when we feel better than those whose addictions
are not fashionable.
The drug addict at least is aware that he is addicted;
are you aware
that you are a junkie?

In Flux

Took our culture
so we wouldn't know ourselves;—
took our Gods
so we wouldn't center;—
took our hearts
so we wouldn't love ourselves,
and took our minds
so we wouldn't care.
And now they wonder
why we are,
who we are.

***

The collective black psyche
is a distorted and misshapen thing.
Humanity owes it to itself to fix it.

In Flux

If we cured all the diseases,
how would the people find a way to die?

***

And who do you pray to when life rips at the seam?;
when the American god
is the American dream.

In Flux

And what of capital punishment?
The killing of a man, for the killing of another man.
What does it mean?
On what logic does it lean,
if on any at all?
It would seem that this is the call
of a society whose conscience is small,
who has dropped the ball;
for killing a man, for killing another man,
is killing another man;
is abject confusion,
is a major contradiction.
It is the blind killing the blind
for being blind;
the conclusion of a deranged mind;
myopia of the worst kind.
It is an attempt to end sickness
by demonstrating sickness,
it is the sick killing the sick
for being sick,
a twisted trick,
a crazy and convoluted flick
with an end that's decidedly tragic.

In Flux

Change is a train that does not stop;
that has no station.
Those who seek to hold it back
will either be severely bruised,
or will be dragged to death of frustration.
The train of change does not stop,
it keeps changing gears.

***

There is one constant
in all of existence.
That is change.
Change
will never change.

In Flux

If you are already married,
you probably have lived this already;
if you're not,
there is something you should know.
The person you now know
will rapidly disappear after marriage,
and a monster shall replace him.
If, when the monster appears,
you cannot accept him;
if your "love" cannot transcend his "faults,"
if you cannot see the beauty in his ugliness,
the uniqueness of his imperfection,
then marriage becomes a jail;
a system of correction
that is bound to fail.

In Flux

To make an icon of a dead man is bad;
to make an icon of a living man is worse.
When men make monuments out of men,
and out of men's memories,
men become men that are less than men.
Amen.

***

God knows, I have lived black times;
and being black, I can tell you
that being black doesn't help.

In Flux

Calling a mystic, a mystic,
is naming someone
who seeks to abolish all names.

***

Consider yourself blessed
if in this life you met someone who believed in you,
more than you believed in yourself.

In Flux

It is true that where I am in life sometimes bothers
me;
but I am who I am,
and while I am who I am,
I will accept who I am;
I will love who I am;
I will be who I am;
for I AM.

***

In the language of reality,
love is at once the vehicle, the road,
and the destination.
Love is everything.
Love is All.
Love IS.

In Flux

Hey doc,
thought you were God,
as you no doubt felt;
thought you knew all there was to know about
everything,
as you no doubt knew;
thought you were God, honestly doc,
until I saw wisdom
watching ignorance increase with knowledge.
Thought you were God, doc,
but then I saw the guessing game;
I saw the game of poker you play
with life and death,
and yet,
your face never weeps its hypocrisy;
knew you weren't God, doc,
when I saw half the time
the puzzle work itself out;
when I knew
you hadn't a clue,
but weren't human enough to stop
and wonder;
wish you'd be God, doc,
wish you'd just be,
but ego kills vision,
can never see.
Grow up doc,
you're all I've got
this side of heaven.

In Flux

Success is just the byproduct of what has been
                                        assimilated
    from previous failures;
        either yours,
    or somebody else's.

***

                God
    is not an intellectual pursuit.
        ALL does not surrender
            to analysis
            and logic.

In Flux

Blacks, as a people,
are not scientifically oriented;
science is not our calling.
We are a people of art,
of dance,
of sport,
of music,
of poetry,
of things not contrived.
We are a natural people;
that is who we are.
And since "intelligence" is measured in "scientific"
terms,
we do not, and cannot measure up,
and we shouldn't.
For life is art,
it is not science;
life is liberty,
it is not technology;
life is love,
it is not logic;
life is lived,
it is not dissected and gutted
to find answers that do not exist;
life has no reason
except the greater expression of itself.
Although science does not know it,
the quest of science, is to prove art.
Science seeks to prove
what black people already know.

In Flux

Dying for what you believe,
is actually easier
than living for what you believe.

***

Ego is the creator of time,
and time
is the creator of greed.

In Flux

The irony of the black situation
is that we remain mired in a fear-based theology
that is not our own.
It was forced upon us.
It was used to enslave us.
It has so succeeded, that even now,
while those who gave it to us are rejecting it,
we have adopted it as our own.

***

The only exam worth taking
is your self exam.
The rest
are a worthless test.
They mean nothing.

In Flux

The greatest irony of the concept of society,
is that the blindest among us
lead us.

***

The men whose books
would be the greatest books,
do not write books.
Books are too small.

In Flux

Live your life fully,
for yesterday and tomorrow are illusions.
Live here, live now.
Grant yourself experiences. Make mistakes—
the more, the better.
Know that failure is a tool,
and if you fear it you cannot use it.
Have no fear of failure,
for it is failure if used constructively
that guarantees success.

***

You become a failure
when you believe it;
never before.

In Flux

Relativity is our collaborative creation,
and judgment is the tool with which we maintain it.

***

For what is life
if there is no live in it?
For what is love
if there is no give in it?

In Flux

> Make your own mold,
> cast yourself,
> then destroy it.
> This is so no one uses it
> and cripples himself.

***

> The first law of paradox is,
> to win
> you have to surrender.

How can you want freedom of religion,
and not want freedom in religion?
Isn't that inherently contradictory?

***

In telling us to fear and to love God in the same
breath,
religion asks of us an impossibility.
It is patently impossible
to love what you fear;
love and fear
are light and darkness.
They do not meet.
They cannot meet.
Where one is, the other is absent.

In Flux

> Life is like jazz;
> the more rules you break,
> the sweeter the music.

***

Do not borrow another's clothes unless you have tried
them on
and they fit.
Do not borrow another's philosophy unless you have
lived it,
and have seen that it works for you.

In Flux

And your children,
who have not yet walked barefoot in grass;
who have never rolled around
in the dirt from whence we came;
who have never run naked
in the rain that is our lifeblood;
these children,
how can we expect them to feel
what they do not touch?

In Flux

Construct your own life philosophy;
one that your self is comfortable with
and hold it dear.
Do not, however,
allow it to become a dogma,
to be written in stone,
for dogmas are useless;
they use people, but people cannot use them.
Have some core principles to work with,
and you can add or subtract
as you go along.
Let it, like your life,
be a fluid experience.
Let it be an unfolding.

Marijuana is not a gateway drug;
it does not yet have that distinction.
Our gateway drugs are currently all legal.

***

Addiction is a mind-body conspiracy
with a phenomenal memory.
The key is to either unravel the conspiracy,
or to kill the memory.

In Flux

If I were to die today,
I would have but one regret.
My regret would be,
that I had not yet learned to live
what I "know."

***

I read somewhere
that love is an act of will;
not true.
Love starts
where will ends.

In Flux

Those who still believe
that God cares about sexual orientation,
are still confused.
Perfection
has never had one orientation.

***

Religion has lost its way.
If you look deeply
you will see the asymmetry.
God is symmetry.

In Flux

     I went
   to one of those churches;
   don't remember where,
   don't remember when;
    when I was young;
    when I knew it all.
  And what I saw was nothing new;
what I heard was of the same color—
    maybe a different hue;
  but of what I felt, I hadn't a clue;
   a curious sort of deja vu,
of you meeting you on a bolt of lightning,
    in a black spiritual.
     That church
    has my number.

In Flux

I have often dreamt
of living in a house without walls,
in a yard without fences;
of living in a country without borders,
among people with no language
and no color;
of seeing,
without the limitation of vision;
of knowing,
without the encumbrance of thought.

***

If you can be defined,
you are not living.
You are dead.

In Flux

We apply laws and rules that do not change,
to an existence that is ever changing.
We are applying the dead to the living,
and expecting harmony.
We are applying nonsense to sense,
and hoping it somehow makes sense.

***

Our laws were made to serve us;
that was supposed to be their function.
Our laws now, however,
only serve themselves.
We have become slaves to our laws.
When laws become edicts and dogmas,
they become what edicts and dogmas ultimately
                                          become,
purposeless.

In Flux

Take time alone daily with yourself;
examine your life;
ask questions—
the tougher, the better.
The answers you may not always like,
but accept them,
they are who you are.
To grow,
to become,
to go forth,
you have to know where you are located,
and to accept that location.
So pose tough questions.

In Flux

Belief in God means nothing;
it is just a mind concept;
it is just another ego vitamin.
God lives outside of both belief
and disbelief.

***

The term "open mind," is an oxymoron.
Mind by its very nature
is closed.

Gandhi and Mandela
were not politicians.
Lambs amongst wolves
are still lambs
amongst wolves.
These men have afforded the contrast
for the darkness that is politics.
Is light
a component of darkness?

***

Cuba, proportionately,
may have done more for the Third World
than all of the developed world combined.
And Cuba
is a monster nation.

In Flux

We see ourselves creating every day,
yet is never occurs to us
that we might be Gods;
that we, in fact, might be who we have been searching
for,
yearning for, all our collective lives.
That idea is too frightening
for us to contemplate.

***

Selflessness
is born of selfishness.
If you have not found you,
how can you find me?

In Flux

Ain't no hurt,
ain't no dread,
when you live inside your head.
Ain't no growth,
ain't no gain,
when you live outside of pain.
Ain't no structure,
ain't no scheme,
when you live inside your dream.
Ain't nothing but clouds of dust
that swirl and drift,
and touch nothing,
and is touched by nothing.
Ain't nothing
when everything amounts to nothing.

In Flux

Compassion is not only putting on another's shoes;
it is to walk in them;
it is to be chafed by them;
it is to feel the road through the holes
in the soles of them.
Compassion means
owning another's shoes.

***

Those who have won the world
and lost their souls,
at least have the world.
What of those who have won nothing,
and are soulless?

In Flux

But the sky never changes;
and night follows day, and day follows night
like a frictionless wheel that spins into oblivion.
Flowers still bloom in spring,
and lovers still kiss;
children still play the same inane games
of hopscotch and double dutch;
and birth and death
have not paused in their eternal quest
to outdo each other.
Yet somewhere I read, that nature was ever changing,
ever dynamic,
ever different,
from the last moment to the next.
An interplay of atoms and electrons
and God knows what.
An invisible tapestry
that bends and shifts,
and stretches,
and breaks,
and mends again,
and touches me,
and touches you,
and the homeless man you may never know.

In Flux

There will come a time
when people will stop voting.
They will still their voice.
They will still their voice,
so politicians can hear themselves;
so they can hear the emptiness;
so they can hear the deceit;
so they can hear,
that people are beginning to care.

***

My definition of assisted suicide,
is the relationship that the World bank and the I.M.F.
have
with the Third World.

The value of history
is greatly overrated.
History has been so corrupted,
so distorted,
so manipulated,
that its value
is questionable at best.
History is not truth.
Tread very carefully
through the minefield of history books.

***

Logic taken to extremes
is often a lie.

In Flux

Sometimes I want to grab the world
by its crazy tail,
and wring it dry of its misery;
then cry in public
for days,
and water it with tears
of joy.
It wouldn't be enough.
It couldn't be enough.

***

The reason there aren't more success stories,
is that we don't allow them to happen.
We do not give people second chances.

Growth has four phases.
In the first, one is unconscious;
one is thought.
One judges, and cannot see outside of that judgment;
one is that judgment.
This is thought.

In the second, one is conscious;
one recognizes his independence from thought.
One judges, but recognizes that one has judged
after judgment has occurred, and hence one can
release that judgment.
This is afterthought.

In the third, one is above thought;
one is aware.
One does not judge, for one preempts the thought
that would judge.
This is forethought.

In the fourth, there is no thought,
and hence no judgment;
no possibility of judgment.
Thought becomes knowing.
This is no-mind.
This is the mind of God.

In Flux

Somebody said
that if you forget your history,
you were doomed to live it again.
We have built countless monuments to our history,
and we keep reliving the same idiocies.
Maybe we should just forget our history
and see what happens.

***

It is an insult
that some whites do not listen to jazz,
for the sole reason that they perceive it as black
music.
It is an insult
that some blacks do not listen to country music,
for the sole reason that they perceive it as white
music.
It is neither an insult to blacks
nor to whites;
they are not important.
It is an insult to music.
It is the music of lovemaking that brought us here,
and during our stay, it is the music that keeps us
sane;
and it is music that accompanies us home again.
Music will be here
after both black and white disappear.

In Flux

If I don't mess up every now and again;
if I don't occasionally cause them some pain,
how will my friends demonstrate their love?
How will they validate themselves
if I never give them the opportunity?

***

The most frustrating aspect of raising children
is what I call double madness.
You get mad at your child,
then you get mad, for getting mad.

In Flux

Politics, as is practiced, dehumanizes people.
When your life becomes shaped
by what people think about you;
by what the newspapers say about you;
by what the polls suggest;
by what decisions are popular and which are not;
by where and with whom one can be seen;
by what and when one can say what,
one ultimately loses touch with oneself.
One's opinion becomes whatever is popular,
and one's beliefs become whatever is "politically
correct."
This is self alienation.
This is prostitution of self.
This is neurosis.
Politicians ultimately become people who have no
idea
who they are, or what they stand for.

In Flux

Dream,
even if that is all you do;
what can be wrong with that?

***

Mistakes are only mistakes
when you make the same ones twice;
outside of that,
they are teaching aids.

In Flux

The practice of demanding apologies
is an absurdity.
Apologies on demand are no longer apologies;
they are coercions.
They mean nothing.

***

Aren't those who cheer when a killer is sentenced to
death
just as sick as he is?

In Flux

The fire went out under the dream,
and the dream went cold
and stiff;
so the dream died.
The dream died,
but was never buried
and so became a wish.
And wishes,
being inherently empty,
having no skeleton,
have no form or meaning.
So the wish imploded into its void
and so became hot air,
that rose,
and stayed suspended between worlds.
In that place where no dreams exist,
there are no dreams to thaw.

In Flux

To hate hate,
is to perpetuate fear;
for what is hate
but fear that does not know itself?

***

This straight and narrow path of which they preach;
this path paved with dogmas,
and rules,
and regulations
and restrictions
and self denials
leads nowhere.
It is a blind alley.
It's only value lies in the walking of it,
and seeing for yourself that it leads to a barren
wilderness.

In Flux

This may surprise you my child,
but I have no problem with you getting married for
money.
None whatever.
You can touch, see, and spend it;
you know that the greens
and the means,
are why you're there.
You're clear.
Never ever, however,
get married because of sympathy, guilt, loneliness,
or the need to feel validated by another.
Over time, they become lost in the shuffle,
and resentment and misery haunt your life,
foster strife,
and you have no clue from whence it comes.

In Flux

Love those who hate you,
for they are only blind people.
How can you blame the blind
for being blind?
That in itself
would be blindness.

***

Life was supposed to be a game,
a sacred game.
We have made it into a con game,
a farce,
a lie.

In Flux

The greats of art,
and dance,
and music,
and sports,
are those who think the least
while they are on the job.

***

Logic says
that seeing is believing;
wisdom says
that seeing is knowing.

In Flux

And they tell us that science and technology
will solve all our problems;
that we will live longer;
that we will own more;
that we will know more.
We will live longer,
so we can hate each other longer.
We will own more,
so we can be less.
We will know more,
so we'll be more ignorant of our idiocy.
No problem.

***

The good teacher
does not provide answers.
The good teacher
provides problems;
creates uncertainty;
fosters inquiry.
Finding answers
is the student's job.

In Flux

How could lobbying be legal,
and prostitution illegal?
How could institutionalized bribery be legal,
and individual freedom be illegal?
How could societal rape be legal,
and consensual money-sex be illegal?
Are we walking on our heads?

***

Why do we beg excuses after burping or farting,
and not after smiling or pissing?
Are they not all natural bodily functions?
Are some holier than others,
or does it have something to do with gas?

In Flux

Sit, my son,
on these grasses that you take for granted;
listen, my son,
to the winds that you take for granted;
they say that life, like you and me,
is a paradox;
it says things it doesn't mean,
and means things it doesn't say;
and says and means things we may never
understand.
Its difficult lessons are simple,
for they simply say that the things that matter
are not material,
and that material things, are in fact immaterial.
If this makes no sense, that's okay;
when it does,
you become a man,
but to grow
you have to remain a child.

In Flux

When people fail to believe in people,
people fail.

***

I read somewhere
that love has no purpose,
except to perpetuate itself.
That is beautiful.

In Flux

Cherish your enemies.
They are a blessing,
not in disguise.

***

Do not ever seek to live up to anyone's expectations,
for that is a prison;
anyone who demands that you do
could not possibly love you.
They seek
to make a slave of you.

In Flux

Accept others for who they are,
and not for who you want them to be.
Judge no one, and as importantly,
do not judge yourself.
Do not waste your energy analyzing the motives of
others,
for it will depress you;
see the good in others,
and encourage it;
see the imperfection in others,
and bless it;
for one could not exist in the absence of the other.
Live optimism, embody it.
Live your life as an example,
but do not stretch yourself to please others.
Live a life of your own dictate;
ignore whoever suggests otherwise.

In Flux

Love is all there is;
nothing else is true,
however real
it may look or feel.

***

There are only two places you will find passionate
people;
at the top of their craft,
or in the cemetery.
They either succeed grandly,
or they die trying to.

In Flux

All that spirituality means,
is an end to bullshittin;
both yourself,
and those around you.

***

Love does not mean loyalty.
Truth cannot be sacrificed
for loyalty.

In Flux

         Logic
is the enemy of wisdom.
Logic says
that love is not possible without conditions;
wisdom says
that once there are conditions,
there is no love.
Logic says
that giving is equal to loss,
for if you give what you have,
what do you in fact have?
Wisdom says
give all,
for who could you give to but yourself?
Logic says
life is war;
wisdom says
life is child's play.
Logic says
that what you see and touch
is what is;
wisdom says
that what is
is what we do not see,
abd what we have not touched.
Logic
is the man who is proud of his achievements;
wisdom is the man
that laughs knowingly at his.

If you take a step back from life,
you will come to the conclusion that life is nonsense;
it is only if you take another step back,
can you see the beauty and the genius in the
nonsense.

***

If you fear what you seek,
how in the world will you find it?
How can you find God
if you fear God?

In Flux

It is not possible to create what you do not want.
We must want drugs, for drugs are here;
why then, are we demonizing drugs?
We are denying our creations when they do not serve
us.
We are disowning our children,
when they seem too ugly to us.
That is tragic.

***

We learn little from winning,
but we love it.
We learn a great deal from losing,
but we hate it.
The message is clear;
we hate learning.

In Flux

The second law of paradox is that,
to know,
you have to give up knowledge;
to know,
you have to not know;
to know,
you have to suspend thought and judgment;
to know,
you have to unknow;
to know,
you have to become a child again.

***

Time is thought;
time is the projection of thought;
ego is thought;
ego, therefore, being thought, is time.
If ego and time are one and the same,
who are we?
Are we not just time keepers?

In Flux

The abused, they never look in,
for fear of what they will not find.
The abusers, they never look in,
for fear of what they will find.
They both look out,
at each other, at nothing.
They are both beggars,
how can they begin to be of any help to each other?

***

When mind begins to question itself,
when ego begins to question its own authenticity,
All is at hand.

In Flux

The education of our children
should be a journey of discovery,
and not a culture of imposition.
It should be a quest
to unearth the innate gifts in our children,
and to nurture them.
That, and only that,
should be the mandate of any system of education.
What we currently have
is a system of systematic indoctrination;
of being fed and asked to regurgitate others' opinions,
of having no questions and no opinions.
Our system of education produces a genre of human
that toes the line and looks up for instruction;
that has neither independent thought nor
spontaneity;
a conditioned reflex
that protects the status quo,
for the status quo is all he can know.
Our system of education is uniquely designed
to produce slaves.

In Flux

The most potent mind altering and addicting drug
is in your living room;
your color t.v.
We actively promote addiction,
then wonder where our addicts come from.

***

Those who believe they know,
can sometimes be more convincing
than those who do.

In Flux

When the word love is used as a noun
it becomes an obscenity.
Love is so alive;
love is so much a process,
that calling love a thing is an insult to the
intelligence
that is love.
Love can love with such love
that love can love any hidden love
out of exile.
I love it.

***

It is only when academia replaced commonsense
that the world became screwed up.

In Flux

And the Catholics hate the Protestants,
and the Protestants hate them back.
And the Christians hate the Jews.
And the Jews hate the Muslims,
And the Muslims hate them back;
and the beat goes on.
And the Agnostics scratch their heads in
                            bewilderment,
for they all call what they practice,
religion.

***

There must come a time in all our lives,
when we stop quoting others.
Life is ultimately
about making your own quotes.

In Flux

So long as district attorneys are allowed
to seek political office;
so long as their competence is measured
by the number of convictions they make,
and not by their passion for truth;
so long as their campaign declarations of toughness
on crime
are met with cheers,
while they have nothing to say about justice;
our innocent poor will continue to fill our jails
and our cemeteries.

***

Nothing that is important
can be taken away from you.
It is just not possible.

In Flux

Ever thought to yourself
on one of those quaint, quiet days,
who invented music?
Who has the rights to these hearts
that we've borrowed?
Must have been some crazy, funky dude,
in love with himself and life,
and felt like dancing with the mud and dust
that made us.
Must have been a woman.
Must have been
a black woman.

Begging is probably the toughest profession.
If you are well groomed,
people say you look better than them;
that you should go get a job;
they never, however,
suggest where to look or how.
If you look dirty and unkept,
they say you're a druggie and want their money
to buy drugs.
It seems it never occurs to them
that even if you were a druggie, that druggies also
eat.
If you look physically strong,
they tell you to go catch lions,
cut cane, or fight Mike Tyson.
Begging is the toughest profession
because people will always find a reason
to not give.

In Flux

How could learned men declare
that they are pro-life,
and support the death penalty?
That is either intellectual dishonesty,
or just plain confusion.
Something is very wrong with that picture.

***

Supporters of the death penalty are essentially saying
that adult humans are not redeemable;
even God almighty
has never made such an assertion.

In Flux

How can we have happy marriages,
when prejudice discounts three quarters of our
possibilities?
If we limit our partner possibilities by race,
by religion,
by culture,
by social status,
by physical attributes,
and by ideologies,
what do we have left?
Marriage is a gamble to begin with,
so why would one eliminate that many possibilities at
the outset?
What we practice,
any professional gambler will tell you,
is an absurdity.

In Flux

How could minds that could conceive the
                                            inconceivable,
that could know the impossible,
not figure out a way to end world hunger?
How could they have gone to the moon,
while children die too soon,
nothing in their spoon?
How could minds so big not see,
that this is certified insanity?
And we call them geniuses.

***

If you don't meet yourself,
how can you know?
If you don't confront yourself,
how can you grow?

In Flux

The greatest athletes
are not those that perform in the olympics
and the world cups.
The greatest athletes
are those who can most skillfully walk the tightrope
between this world and the next.
The greatest athletes
are those who live the absolute
within the relative.
The greatest athletes
are those who choose to live within limits,
while knowing that they are limitless.

***

Politics is a lie,
for its premise is a lie.
Politics presupposes that we the people
cannot handle truth.

In Flux

If you strive to be better than the rest,
you are lost.
If you strive to be the best that you can be,
you will be found.
If you have no striving,
you are found.
You are home.
You are free.

***

Isn't it strange
that those who live in primitive societies are human,
and we,
who live in "civil" societies are animals?

In Flux

From the ashes of a culture scattered on ill winds,
rise fragments of who I am;
pieces of a puzzle forever lost
in history's white jungle.
I am, therefore, not complete,
found wanting
in that which is the me in me.
I am, therefore,
a semicircle that cannot arch to completion;
an unfulfilled lover;
an idea yearning to be born;
from an embryo of schizophrenic and bankrupt
thought processes;
a tree that will never flower;
minutes that will never hour.

In Flux

Stress is largely a self-imposed condition.
It is a type of self mutilation
that is done in a somnambulistic state.
If is a deferred, unconscious suicide.

***

Racism is a kind of neurosis;
an ego driven form of false self aggrandizement,
of self illusion.
It is a form of self denial,
for if you deny your brother, you deny yourself.
A racist is not whole.
A racist is counterfeit.
Racism ultimately
is confusion masquerading as conviction.

In Flux

The minds of most humanity are prisons;
black minds, however,
are maximum security prisons.
Prisons within prisons.
Prisons,
locked solid with fear;
prisons,
locked solid for lack of repair;
prisons of rust,
of dust,
of mistrust.
Ours is a prison built by others,
but we do the maintenance.
We keep it current.

In Flux

Negative is as positive,
as positive is positive.
Positive owes its existence to negative.
Negative is positive.

***

If, as some claim, the cause of racism is ignorance, why does it exist in our so called institutions of higher learning?
What does this say about our system of education?

In Flux

While science dreams
of a theory of everything,
saints are busy living it.

***

There are some of us
that even God cannot please.
In winter we hate the cold.
In summer we hate the heat.
In spring we can't handle the allergies,
and in fall we can't handle the rain.
Ain't that a pain?

In Flux

It matters not
what you think of me.
After all, the you that would judge me
is not real;
and the me that would be offended
is as equally unreal.
It is the case of a lie
that seeks to negate another lie,
so as to perpetuate the central lie.

***

If as a manager,
you are feared by your subordinates;
even if you are getting the job done,
you are not doing your job.

In Flux

I am convinced
that death is not our greatest fear.
Our greatest fear is ourselves.
We are terrified to look at, and to accept ourselves.
Many of us have committed suicide;
many of us have chosen death,
over looking at, and accepting ourselves.

***

Hate is an emotion that is so absurd,
there is actual beauty
in its perverse stupidity.
Hate is immaculately idiotic.

In Flux

People who kill people, outside of self defense and
accidentally,
are sick people.
And we kill these people.
We kill our sick
and claim we are a compassionate society.
And people who are suffering in agony and request to
die,
are ignored.
We prolong life in those who wish to die,
and against their wishes;
and we claim we are a free society.

***

The world is peopled by three people.
He who knows. He is rare. He has no opinion.
He who thinks he knows. He is commonplace. He is
full of opinions,
most of which are meaningless.
And he who believes that he who thinks he knows
actually does.
He is the masses. He also has no opinion.

In Flux

If there was a manual for life,
the only happy people
would be the illiterate ones.

***

The great men are those
who have captivated the collective consciousness of
humanity.
They range from the all loving, to the "evil" and
"repugnant."
The narrow minded among us will never legitimize
the "negative" greatness of a man;
they cannot see the gift he brings in outstretched
hand.
They cannot see the opportunity he presents
for us to demonstrate our goodness, our love, our
compassion.
Without opportunity and choice,
who are we?

In Flux

Politics is a schizophrenic boardgame
that is played mostly under the table,
by blind men.

***

He who questions and seeks his own experience,
will know.
He who believes without inquiry,
and without seeking his own experience,
will never know.
Beliefs are not truths;
beliefs seek validation.
Beliefs are borrowed garbage that serve no purpose
except to cloud the psyche.
Seek experience and discard beliefs.
When you know,
what is the purpose of believing?

In Flux

Even if evil were a fact,
love would still have no equal.

***

My head is me,
but my foot is equally me.

In Flux

Drug addicts
are broken people.
If you look into the lives of most of them,
you will see
sexual/physical/psychic abuse;
abandonment,
love denial,
homophobic experiences,
rejection,
and frank inhumanity.
In short,
we created our addicts;
we as a society drove these people to drugs.
And when they become addicts,
we ostracize them;
we marginalize them to the fringe of society;
we jail them for using the only thing that gives
comfort to them,
for both religion and society failed them.
So,
we created our addicts through abuse and neglect,
and we nurture them with cruelty, condescension, and
discrimination.
And that is the extent of the insanity
in a civil society.

In Flux

He who knows
will tell you that he is God,
that you are God,
that God is God,
that there is no God,
and that all is God
in the same sentence and make sense.

***

Throughout history,
those that we call geniuses
were either never schooled,
dropped out of school,
received alternative schooling,
or did not do well in the traditional school system.
Hmmm...What is there to learn here?

In Flux

You have not yet lived, if you have not
questioned your beliefs,
given yourself totally to something,
broken any law,
loved for no reason,
farted in public,
spoken truth to power,
felt like killing somebody,
spent time with a child,
witnessed a birth and a death.

***

The strong among us
are those who recognize their weaknesses
and acknowledge them.

In Flux

What do you say
to he who says that poverty is necessary,
that poverty has its place,
that poverty and disenfranchisement as a culture
has given to the world most of its great men?
How can one seek to eradicate a culture
that has spawned the best among us?

***

The negativity you see in your brother,
is just your projection unto him of what it is that is
negative in you.
Your brother
is your mirror;
the distorted image you see in him,
is in fact, you.

In Flux

The theory of life is simple,
whatever makes you tick,
tick it (..√..).

***

You are only free
when fear is a vague memory.

In Flux

I come
as I came,
with nothing,
no future and no past,
for the past is a lie,
and the future is a projected lie.
I come with no ambition and no history;
nothing precedes me,
and nothing succeeds me;
I am free.
I come with no philosophy,
for philosophies are ultimately all empty—
empty houses of great design,
new bottle, stale wine.
I go
as I came,
with nothing,
no regrets and no dreams,
no guilt and no schemes;
no regrets,
for a life fully lived has no space for regrets;
and no dreams,
for if you have lived all of it,
what is there to dream about?

In Flux

There are two fundamental forces that determine the evolution of humanity.
The society's attempt to restrict and contain consciousness,
and consciousness itself, which is inherently free.
Consciousness naturally seeks expression and expansion,
while society seeks to deny or retard expansion.
This is manifested as resistance to change, suspicion of the new,
worship of the old, and laws ad nauseam.
It is impossible for society to win in this ridiculous struggle,
but struggle we will.
We can resist change, that is always an option,
stopping it is just not possible.

Heaven is self discovery;
hell is the road that leads there.

***

On matters that really matter,
the majority has rarely ever been right.

In Flux

If people are treated like people,
then people will be people;
they have no choice.

***

The reason we are blind,
is that what we see
is inside our heads;
it is a projection.
Those who really see
have nothing in their heads;
so there is nothing to project.
What they see, is, and is hence alive.
What we see, was, and is hence dead.

In Flux

Leaders are all born;
they are not made.
Only followers are made.
We were all born leaders;
it is our environment, vis a vis family and society,
that made followers of us.
It is only those of us that have been beaten down
that become followers,
and that sadly, is the majority of us.
The follower is the result of abuse of the
mind/body/spirit complex.
The follower is laden with imposed fear, doubt, and
insecurities;
he is a beaten and confused man.
Leaders are either people that were raised in a
nurturing environment,
or that rare breed of human that grew up under the
worst conditions imaginable,
but was never touched by it;
it didn't grow on him.
By leaders, I don't mean politicians and power
trippers,
for they are just as confused as the rest of us;
by leaders, I mean people who know their truth,
and who live it unabashedly and unreservedly;
by leaders, I mean people who know that power is
inherent,
and that the sharing of it is what announces its
reality;
(continued)

In Flux

by leaders, I mean people who encourage others
to find and to live their truth.
In short,
leaders are people who make leaders of people,
by showing them that they are really fallen leaders.
Leaders are really normal people;
followers are damaged people.
When followers are healed
they automatically become leaders.
When all are healed, then all are leaders,
then there are no leaders.
Leadership is not teachable. It is only knowable.

In Flux

Tomorrow
is our collective fear.
Tomorrow is only possible
because of our collective anxiety.
We fear tomorrow's possibilities,
and so give tomorrow its existence.
If the world—
the human collective—
if we were to, on an agreed upon day,
just stop;
stop working,
stop planning,
give up ideas of security,
go fishing,
run naked in the park with your lover—
or someone you don't even know,
just go with the flow;
go on a cruise,
forget the news—
for there won't be any anyway,
everyone would be at play;
go to a party that's happenin,
you and your crew,
make love the entire day wherever you feel like it—
who would give a shit?
The cops would be doin it.
Or go watch a game live—
your favorite game,
play hopscotch or double dutch,

(continued)

In Flux

or just bullshit all day, and such.
In short,
do whatever you wanted to do, however ridiculous or
extravagant,
but time or societal judgments did not permit it.
In short,
become a child again for a day.
If we were to become children again for a day,
tomorrow would disappear;
the unreality of tomorrow would become apparent;
time as we know it
would stop.

In Flux

The concept of ownership
has totally deluded humanity.
Ownership is possible
of only one kind,
ownership of self.
And the greatest irony
is that the only ownership that is possible
we choose not to claim.
We have chosen instead
to "own" things and titles,
bills and baubles.
Ownership has been so perverted
that men have actually believed
that men could own men;
that men could own women;
that men and women could own children.

***

And so our children,
who are only guilty of being innocent,
must endure our abuse and manipulation
to support our twisted ego needs.

In Flux

Societal negativities are necessary,
for they present opportunity;
and opportunity is the substrate of growth.
Were it not for apartheid,
how would we have known the magnitude of
Mandela?
Would we even have heard of him?
Were it not for racism in America,
how would we have known the courage of King?
Would we even have heard of him?

In Flux

It is arrogance
to question the competence of the next generation.
To question the next generation,
is to question existence,
is to question universal intelligence,
is to question God.
In questioning the next generation,
we are questioning the intelligence of the whole
of which we are just a part;
we are saying that the body is wrong,
and we, the asshole of the body, know better.
My take on this is,
if our youth all turn out to be bums,
then their lives will just be a beautiful bump.
It's all good. It's all God.

In Flux

If the white child isn't told,
either in words, actions, pictures, media, or societal
structure itself,
that the black child is less than him,
he wouldn't know it.
It is difficult, if not impossible,
for the white child to believe that the black child is
his equal,
and vice-versa.
There is just too much out there that says otherwise.

***

If no one tells you that you are ugly,
how would you know it?

In Flux

And it will become more and more apparent
that these guys,
these straight "A" guys,
these guys who know it all
and show it all,
are becoming the C.E.O.s of companies owned by
those guys;
the class clowns,
the dropouts,
the expelled troublemakers,
the "D" and "F" caretakers,
the backbenchers,
the duffers,
those guys.

In Flux

The greatest forms of art
are those that do not propose anything;
they ask questions;
they ask deep and haunting questions.
Their intrigue lies in the freedom they give
for answers to be concocted.

***

America
is all business.
Media is business.
Sport is business.
Music is business.
Marriage is business.
Healthcare is business.
Religion and politics are also business,
but hey,
that's none of your business.